How To Write Your Story of Accomplishment And Personal Success

A Story Starter Guide & Workbook to Write & Record Your Business or Personal Goals & Achievements

By Melanie Johnson & Jenn Foster

Melanie Johnson & Jenn Foster

©2016 Elite Online Publishing
63 East 11400 South Suite #230
Sandy, UT 84070
info@bookwritingretreats.com

ISBN: 1523287047
ISBN-13: 978-1523287048

DEDICATION

To our children! You inspire us every day! We are very proud of your accomplishments and success!

TABLE OF CONTENTS

ACKNOWLEDGMENTS

Our Kids,
Nathan & Justice, for always pushing me and encouraging to do more and be better and keeping me on my toes !! I'm thankful every day that you are my sons.
Bailey, Carson & Brendan, for your patience and support for my business. You help me understand the meaning of life! I feel so blessed to have you all in my life.

Our families, for all the support, love and standing by us through thick and thin.

Mike Koenigs, thank you for inspiring us to become authors and start our publishing business.

Chris & Pam Hendrickson, thanks for all your motivational videos and products. We love seeing you speak on stage!

Paul Colligan, thank you for inspiring and encouraging us to be brave enough to start our own podcast.

Darren Hardy, thank you for your daily inspirational emails. You push us to do better and better each day.

Tony Robbins thank you for giving us strategies to make life easier.

And everyone else we may have forgotten to give thanks and praise to. We Thank you Very Much!

INTRODUCTION

"If my doctor told me I had only 6 months to live, I'd type a little faster."

– Isaac Asimov

If you have wanted to write a book of your life's journey you have come to the right place. Did you know that 80% of people want to write a book and become an Author? But only 1 % actually do it. We are going to show you some of our formula that has had success year after year, book after book when YOU IMPLEMENT. We are going to show how to get the results you want. The key is to IMPLEMENT!

You are going to learn what we have found to be the single most powerful way to tell your life story and leave a legacy for family and friends. You will be leaving a slice of history by sharing your personal journey. The **"Accomplishment Story Starter"** will turn your stories and memories into a book.

Our big promise is to help you turn your ideas into a book within 60 days. When you read through this story starter guide, you will see how easy it is. You're going to see and <u>know</u> that by using our workbook and questions, you will be able to do it! You may say, "But I'm not a writer."

WHAT IF I CAN'T WRITE?

You can be an author without having to be a writer. The big important idea behind this is pretty simple. I'm going to show why this is important.

We know that by using our tools, systems and story starters, You too can write a book. This really, really works.

Here are some of the books that were written using some or all of our formula.

- **Video Marketing For Professionals**
- **Books To Bucks**
- **Forgiveness Through Redemption**
- **What You Don't Expect When Becoming a Young Mother**
- **Mindset to Millionaire**
- **Dominican Republic Lifestyle Holiday Vacation Club FAQ's**

- **Enthusiastic YOU!**

There are over 400 authors who have used similar tools and systems. Some of these authors had never written a book before and don't like to write. It's time to put the story of your life into a book to share for lifetimes to come.

You may be saying,

"Gosh, I have a bunch of notes and journals and I just don't know how to put it all together!" Have you started writing a book and are stuck. You can get your book together quickly using our tools and strategies. You will have your book published for years to come and be proud of it.

The First Step

Follow us through the process in this story starter guide and get ready to implement. We are going to lay down a challenge to you: Pick a date right now to have your book written and launched. That will get you committed. Once you have your date, share it. Share it on Facebook, with family or friends or even with one single person that will be an accountability partner for you.

As extra motivation, once your book is done and you choose to publish it, Elite Online Publishing will promote it on our social media. Whether you choose to publish with us or publish your story on your own. That should help encourage you!!!!

How to Write Without Being a Writer

Here are five ways to write a book without being a writer:

1. Talk your book instead of write your book. You can use the app "Evernote" to talk your story and the app will transcribe it as you go.
2. You can talk into your iPhone on "Notes" and it will transcribe it for you.
3. You can video yourself using your phone and a selfie stick and have it transcribed.
4. You can have someone interview you on video using your phone, camera or Google Hangout and have it transcribed.
5. You can hire a ghostwriter to go over the questions with you and write it all down.

TIPS:

- When using Evernote or Notes, you may have to talk slower and more precise, so it will stay up with you. We all tend to talk really fast, so you may have to slow down.

- The cool thing about video is that you can save it for later and upload it to YouTube. You can share it privately to just family and friends or you can share it to the whole world.

- Here are some websites we recommend to find a transcriber:

www.odesk.com

www.elance.com

www.fancyhands.com

www.fiverr.com

Question & Answer

This book is full of questions to get you thinking about the stories in your life. To open up your mind about your business or personal goals and achievements. We want you to share your success with the world. But before you dive in and answer the questions let's get your mindset ready and your brain turned on!

GET YOUR HEAD IN THE GAME

1. **DECLARE YOURSELF A WRITER -** The words "I am" are very powerful. State it as a fact. Act like a writer, talk like a writer and start writing. Remember you become what you focus on.

2. **BE OPEN** - Allow yourself to be open to getting out of your comfort zone, accepting all forms of criticism, and overcoming your fears and inhibitions. Be Vulnerable. Here is a great TED talk on being Vulnerable http://0s4.com/r/BROWN

3. **EVERYDAY-** Do something that moves you toward your goal of getting your book done everyday. It may not even be writing. You may research or observe something, or take a few notes. It's the compound effect. It all adds up.

4. **KNOW YOUR WHY-** You have to know the reason why you are writing your book. What is your purpose? What do you want the outcome to be? How do you want your readers to feel after they read your book? What lessons, benefits or insights will they gain?

5. **VISUALIZE-** Picture how you will feel once you have told your story. Imagine what it's like to have completed sharing your legacy, story, knowledge and wisdom. Visualize how others will react once they know you have written a book. Visualize how the readers will feel and their expressions after they have read your book.

6. **PLACES**- Pick a special place to write or record your book. It can be a place that is special to you or that is quiet, where you can focus.

7. **SET A DEADLINE**- We challenged you in the paragraph above to set a date and share it with others. Most people work best with a deadline, so set your date and make it happen.

8. **NEVER GIVE UP-** If for some reason you miss your deadline or you are still sitting with this workbook on your desk and you haven't implemented, don't beat yourself up, just try again. Today is a new day and the perfect day to get started.

MINDSET MAKEOVER

HAPPY DAYS ARE HERE AGAIN!

Here are some great ways to get in a positive mindset before you write your book. Practice all or some of these. Not only will they put you in a great mood to write your book, they will improve your every day life. Happiness is a choice, choose it everyday!!!!

1. **Gratitude-** When you feel there should be more to life, take an inventory of what you already have. Your health, family, friends, a place to live, clothes to wear, food to eat, your skills and your dreams.

2. **Giving-** This makes us happier and healthier and it creates stronger connections between

people. You can give your time, your ideas and your smile.

3. **Exercising-** Take care of your body; it's the only one you've got. The body and mind are connected. Being active makes us happier, improves our mood, helps us sleep better and gives us a strong energetic body.

4. **Live in the Moment-** Appreciate the world around you, even noticing the breeze rustling the leaves on a tree.

5. **Grow-** Keep learning new things. It gives us a sense of accomplishment and improves our well being. It helps us stay curious and engaged.

6. **Have Goals-** This gives us something to look forward to. Feeling good about our future is important for happiness. Goals excite us and motivate us. They give us direction.

7. **Emotion-** Research shows that regularly experiencing joy, gratitude, contentment, inspiration and pride creates an upward momentum in our spirit.

8. **Acceptance-** Love who you are. Be kind to yourself. Don't dwell on who you are not or compare yourself to others. We each have our unique gifts and talents and we should celebrate each other.

9. **Purpose and Meaning-** Be a part of something bigger. Leave a legacy and tell your story. People who have meaning and purpose in their lives are happier and live longer.

10. **Motivation-** Find your "Why". It could be a goal, something you love, something you hate, or something you are passionate about.

11. **Journaling-** This releases the thoughts from the day or week. This helps us reflect and release everything that is rattling around in our head and put it down on paper.

12. **Gratitude Journal-** Write down the 5-10 things you are grateful for each day. Oprah says doing this one thing will change your life.

13. **Read or Listen to Something Inspiring-** Fill your head with positive, healthy, energizing, thoughts. This is health food for the brain.

14. **Meditate or Pray-** Take some quiet time for your mind to be at peace and rest with your creator.

15. **Do an Activity as a Family-** This will bond you together and create a memory.

16. **Perform Random Acts of Kindness-** If you want something you should give it away and

then it will come back to you. If you want love, give love; if you want a mentor, be a mentor.

17. **Create a Vision Board-** Fill this with pictures of things you would like to achieve and experience. Examples are: vacations, cars, trips, and romance.

18. **Wake Up to Happy Music-** Why not start your day on a upbeat, happy note. Pick music that has meaning to you and puts a smile on your face.

19. **Dance Like Nobody's Watching-** Really, turn on some music and go full-tilt crazy dancing. Watch how your mood will change.

20. **Sweet Dreams-** Think of a few things that really make you happy, or something you would like to experience that would put a smile on your face before you go to bed. You are programming your mind for what

you want to dream about. People wake up happier when they have had a happy or positive dream the night before.

21. **Breathe-** Your body is primarily made up of water. It is 70% water and thrives on oxygen. Most of us don't breathe enough, especially if we don't do a great cardio workout. When we are stressed we tend to breathe shallowly. If you are like me, you hold your breath when stressing about things. Here is a quick tip. Take 10 deep breaths in for 4 seconds, holding each one for 4 seconds, then breath out for 6 seconds. Do this 3 times a day. Do it in the morning, in your car, while you are walking the dog, and lying in bed before you go to sleep. You will have more energy and be more relaxed and your mind will think more clearly.

22. **Eat Well-** Water, water, water! 70% of your diet should contain water rich foods. That means fruits and vegetables. Try this exercise; write down what you ate for the last 24 hours and see how much of it came from the earth versus prepackaged.

23. **You Are The Company You Keep-** Stay away from the character Eeyore from Winnie The Pooh. Even though you're happy an energized attitude will be contiguous. People that live in the black abyss can suck you in. Limit your time from the terminal Eeyore types. Take inventory of the company you keep. Research shows you will start to take on the traits of the company you regularly keep. If they are always eating ice cream, before you know it, you will be eating ice cream with them. If they always use certain words or phrases, you will find

that you start using some of the same words and phrases. (Just saying!)

24. **Give a Compliment-** It's amazing how someone's face will light up when you give them a sincere compliment. What happens afterward is that you get a warm fuzzy feeling inside knowing you have brightened someone's day.

25. **Sleep Your Way to the Top-** Getting enough sleep is imperative. Your brain doesn't function at full speed when you are sleep deprived. There is nothing pretty about being burnt out and exhausted.

26. **Eat an Apple a Day-** The saying is NOT eat a cookie a day. Think of the small stuff and the compound effect over time it will have. What if you did replace that cookie or cupcake with an apple or a piece of fruit? What would the result be after one week,

one month, one year? It's the small things that will make a major difference in your life.

27. **Smile, DAMN IT!** - The best way to immediately reduce stress is to SMILE. Your body naturally relaxes when you smile. Wake up and smile before your feet hit the ground. When you first look into the mirror in the morning smile at yourself. Guess what? You'll be smiling right back at yourself. Isn't it nice to wake up to a happy face?

"Smile - It Increases Your Face Value!"

- Dolly Parton

28. **Give Yourself a Hug-** Literally wrap your arms around yourself and squeeze for a whole minute or so, take a few deep breaths and smile.

29. **Own Happiness, Health and Productivity-** Act Happy, talk like you're happy, walk like you're happy, think like

you're happy, smile like you're happy, dress like you're happy. Put the actions behind your intention and they will become a reality.

30. **P.S. I Love YOU!-** First off, give yourself love. It's not enough to say it in your head. Stand in front of a mirror, look at yourself for about one minute or so in silence, gazing at all that you are and then say, "I Love you, I really love you." This practice has brought some people to tears the first time they do it. Now think of the people you love in your life and mentally send love to them. Then visualize how they will respond and look at you when they feel you love them. Now that's a pretty picture!

"We all have a life story and a message that can inspire others to live a better life or run a better business. Why not use that story and message to serve others"

-Brendon Burchard

Melanie Johnson & Jenn Foster

GOALS

"The future belongs to those who believe in the beauty of their dreams."
-Elenor Roosevelt

1. Describe the event you took place in, or the goal you met.

_____

_____

_____

_____

_____

_____

_____

_____

_____

_____

2. How were you introduced to this event/ goal?

_____

_____

_____

_____

_____

_____

_____

_____

_____

 Accomplishment Story Starter

3. What made you decide to set this goal or participate in the event?

_____

_____

_____

_____

_____

_____

_____

_____

_____

_____

4. Once you thought of the prospect of accomplishing this goal, how long did it take you to really commit to it?

_____

_____

_____

_____

_____

_____

_____

_____

_____

_____

5. Did you write your goal down? Where?
Describe how that made the goal more real.

_____

_____

_____

_____

_____

_____

_____

_____

_____

_____

6. Did you share your goal with anybody?
What was their response?

_____

_____

_____

_____

_____

_____

_____

_____

_____

_____

7. Did you research the opportunity or just "dive in?"

_____

_____

_____

_____

_____

_____

_____

_____

_____

_____

8. Describe your feeling before you started, as you were in the middle of the process and once you completed your goal.

_____

_____

_____

_____

_____

_____

_____

_____

_____

9. Did you have to balance other goals or responsibilities to accomplish your goal?

_____

_____

_____

_____

_____

_____

_____

_____

_____

_____

10. Did you have a mentor that you looked to for success in helping achieve your goal?

_____

_____

_____

_____

_____

_____

_____

_____

_____

_____

MOTIVATION

"Never look where you're going...
always look where you want to go."

-Bob Ernst

1. What was your motivation for accomplishing this goal?

_____

_____

_____

_____

_____

_____

_____

_____

_____

_____

2. How did you stay motivated?

_____

_____

_____

_____

_____

_____

_____

_____

_____

_____

_____

3. Did your motivation stay the same or did it change? How?

_____

_____

_____

_____

_____

_____

_____

_____

_____

4. What did you learn about motivation during this experience?

_____

_____

_____

_____

_____

_____

_____

_____

_____

_____

_____

5. Did you have doubts about accomplishing your goal or did you always feel confident? Did you feel you needed to look confident when you were doubtful?

_____

_____

_____

_____

_____

_____

_____

_____

_____

_____

6. How did you overcome discouragement?

_____

_____

_____

_____

_____

_____

_____

_____

_____

_____

_____

7. Where others motivated by your actions?

_____

_____

_____

_____

_____

_____

_____

_____

_____

_____

_____

8. Were others involved in your motivation?

_____

_____

_____

_____

_____

_____

_____

_____

_____

_____

_____

9. Did promises you made to yourself or others provide motivation? If so, what were those promises?

_____

_____

_____

_____

_____

_____

_____

_____

_____

10. How would you define motivation?

_____

_____

_____

_____

_____

_____

_____

_____

_____

_____

_____

PLANNING

"Whether you think you can or think you can't, you're probably right."
-Henry Ford

1. Did you have a plan for accomplishing your goal?

_____

_____

_____

_____

_____

_____

_____

_____

_____

_____

2. If so, describe the plan in detail.

_____

_____

_____

_____

_____

_____

_____

_____

_____

_____

_____

3. Did you write your plan down or share it with someone?

_____

_____

_____

_____

_____

_____

_____

_____

_____

_____

_____

4. Did you keep track of your plan on a chart or track your progress in some other way?

_____

_____

_____

_____

_____

_____

_____

_____

_____

_____

5. Did your plan change during the process?

_____

_____

_____

_____

_____

_____

_____

_____

_____

_____

_____

_____

6. If so, how? Why?

_____

_____

_____

_____

_____

_____

_____

_____

_____

_____

_____

7. Did you have help creating your plan?

_____

_____

_____

_____

_____

_____

_____

_____

_____

_____

_____

8. Looking back, what were the key parts of the plan that contributes most of your success or failure.

_____

_____

_____

_____

_____

_____

_____

_____

_____

9. Would you have been successful if you did not develop a plan?

_____

_____

_____

_____

_____

_____

_____

_____

_____

_____

10. Was planning easy for you? Did your plan help keep you on course? Did you refer to your plan often?

_____

_____

_____

_____

_____

_____

_____

_____

_____

LESSONS

"The very difficulty of a problem evokes abilities or talents which would otherwise, in happy times, never emerge to shine."
-Horace

1. What lessons did you learn while working on your goal?

_____

_____

_____

_____

_____

_____

_____

_____

_____

2. How was your character developed while working toward your goal?

_____

_____

_____

_____

_____

_____

_____

_____

_____

_____

3. What did you learn about yourself?

_____

_____

_____

_____

_____

_____

_____

_____

_____

_____

4. What did you learn about others?

_____

_____

_____

_____

_____

_____

_____

_____

_____

_____

5. Would you try to accomplish this endeavor again? Why?

_____

_____

_____

_____

_____

_____

_____

_____

_____

_____

6. Was there a time you felt like giving up? What made you change your mind?

_____

_____

_____

_____

_____

_____

_____

_____

_____

7. What encouragement would you give others who wanted to try the same thing?

_____

_____

_____

_____

_____

_____

_____

_____

_____

_____

8. Do you have any regrets about a direction you took? Would you do anything differently?

_____

_____

_____

_____

_____

_____

_____

_____

_____

_____

9. What was your proudest moment during your experience?

_____

_____

_____

_____

_____

_____

_____

_____

_____

_____

10. Was there something that you didn't want to do, but had to do it anyway? How did it turn out?

_____

_____

_____

_____

_____

_____

_____

_____

_____

WHO HELPED MAKE IT HAPPEN

"Interdependence is and ought to be as much the ideal of man as self-sufficiency. Man is a social being." - Gandhi

1. Who helped you accomplish your goal?

_____

_____

_____

_____

_____

_____

_____

_____

_____

_____

_____

2. Who provided support for you? Was their support "active" or "passive"?

_____

_____

_____

_____

_____

_____

_____

_____

_____

_____

3. What did they do to help you succeed?

_____

_____

_____

_____

_____

_____

_____

_____

_____

_____

_____

4. Did others participate in the event or process?

_____

_____

_____

_____

_____

_____

_____

_____

_____

_____

_____

5. If so, who were they? How did they participate?

_____

_____

_____

_____

_____

_____

_____

_____

_____

_____

_____

6. Did anyone discourage or interfere with your plans?

_____

_____

_____

_____

_____

_____

_____

_____

_____

_____

_____

7. What did you learn about the importance of
other people in meeting your goals?

_____

_____

_____

_____

_____

_____

_____

_____

_____

_____

8. Did you feel intimidated by sharing your goals with those close to you?

_____

_____

_____

_____

_____

_____

_____

_____

_____

9. How did your relationships improve as you allowed people close to you to support your experiences?

_____

_____

_____

_____

_____

_____

_____

_____

_____

_____

10. Was anyone envious of your success?

_____

_____

_____

_____

_____

_____

_____

_____

_____

_____

_____

CONCLUSION

Congratulations!!!!! If you are on this page that means you have finished your questions and your book. Way to go!!!!! You are now part of the 1% that write and finish a book. The next step is to edit and publish your book. We suggest you find a good editor or ghostwriter to edit your work. You may have recorded your answers to these questions on audio, if that is the case get your book transcribed. Then send the transcription to your editor. The last step is publishing. We are going to tell you where to publish your book. We publish our clients books for them on these platforms plus many others.

- **Kindle** -This is the first, best, and easiest platform to get recognized on. Amazon promotes your book for you. It pushes you up in the search engines, like Google, Yahoo & Bing.
  Hint: We don't recommend doing KDP Select when you are launching your

book. This gives Kindle 90 days exclusive rights to your book. Meaning you can't give your ebook away during that time.

- **CreateSpace**- Here you can print your book on demand. You can order your books at an extreme discount and have them sent anywhere you want. You can buy 1 or 10,000 so there is no risk or inventory. You can combine your Kindle and CreateSpace together. This allows you to expand to different outlets. It's better to have both the paperback and Kindle versions of your book.

- **Audible**- This is a great way to reach a whole other audience. Some people like to listen to books in their car, while cooking dinner, or even working out. We've done all three of these things.

- **BookBaby** - Sell your eBooks worldwide. BookBaby takes care of all the work. You keep 100% of your net sales. It's the easiest and most robust eBook publishing package on the planet.

Now that you know where to publish. We are going to give you the steps on how to publish it. We can do this for you at Elite Online Publishing or you can do it yourself.

Here we go:

Book Publishing Steps

1. Files

-Book files (ebook file & PDF file 6x9 size).

-Cover graphic files.

-Author biography (Short and Long Version)

2. Book description. (Short and Long Version)

3. Categories.

4. Key words.

5. Upload everything to KDP Amazon for your ebook and Create Space for your print book. (takes about 24-72 hours for approval)

6. Double check categories.

7. Launch! Tell your friends, family, social media & the world that your book is available.

8. Hit #1.

9. Tell the world you are a #1 best-selling author by using social media.

10. Order your paperback books.

11. Launch again when your paperback is ready for shipping.

12. Have a book signing party.

13. Publish your ebook on BookBaby for ebook distribution.

Congratulations NEW AUTHOR!
We at Elite Online Publishing are so proud of you!!!!

"I think I did pretty well, considering I started out with nothing but a bunch of blank paper." – Steve Martin

ABOUT THE AUTHORS

Melanie Churella Johnson is the former owner and Vice President of 2 Independent TV stations in Houston (Channel 51) and Dallas (Channel 55). Melanie has a background in Media, Marketing and Advertising. She has been in front of, as well as behind the camera. Melanie started her career as a News Anchor in Detroit at Channel 20. She is a Michigan native, who graduated from Michigan State University and earned the title of Miss Michigan.

She got her feet wet in the luxury building and design industry when she was the general contractor and developer for her personal 25,000 sq. ft home known as "The Houston Mansion" and her 13,000 sq. ft summer home in Petoskey, Michigan "The Walloon Lake House. "

During the economic down turn, Melanie turned both of these properties into successful Luxury Vacation and Event Rental Properties.

Her newest vacation rental is the Dominican Villa in Puerto Plata. Melanie has traveled all over the world and fell in love with Puerto Plata. She soon purchased a Villa Membership at Lifestyle Holiday Vacation Club. In this book, she shares with you her favorite restaurants and attractions in Puerto Plata. Plus the insider tips to ensure you will have a great time.

If you would like to check out her Vacation Villa Rental go to

www.vrbo.com/263832 or

Email: Melecj@yahoo.com

Other books by Melanie Churella Johnson

Puerto Plata Best Restaurants and Adventures: Insider tips and guide for a great time

Dominican Republic Lifestyle Holiday Vacation Club FAQ's: What You Want to Know Before You Go To Make Your Trip Incredible. Including the Most Frequently Asked Questions and Insider Tips

Book Writing Bible: Expert Secrets on How to Write, Sell, & Market Your Book Online

Jenn Foster is one of today's national leading online and mobile marketing experts. She is the founder and CEO of Biz Social Boom, a company dedicated to helping business owners of all sizes thrive in today's highly technical world of product and service promotion. From local brick and mortar stores to online entities and large international corporations, Jenn's years of experience and expertise has helped hundreds become the front page news on all the major search engines. She is dedicated to helping businesses use powerful new online and mobile marketing platforms to get visibility, traffic, leads, customers and raving fans.

A graduate of Utah State University, Jenn is an award winning web designer, author and sought after speaker. She has been a featured speaker at many local events. She has been on stage as an expert marketing panelist for marketing experts Mike Koenigs, Ed Rush, Paul Colligan and Pam Hendrickson. Jenn has been named one of America's Premier

Experts® and is a co-author in the book Stand Apart with Dan Kennedy, a major national publication, and an Amazon kindle best seller. Jenn recently received a Quilly Award in Hollywood from the National Academy of Best Selling Authors, for her contribution to the book.

When she is not helping her clients, Jenn enjoys spending time with her three children, experiencing the great outdoors and she loves Zumba. Additional information about Jenn and her business can be found at www.JennFosterSEO.net or by texting your email to (801) 901-3480.

Follow Jenn at:
Twitter: @JennFosterChic

Other Books by Jenn Foster:

Stand Apart: Stand Out From the Crowd to Achieve Ultimate Success.
Featuring Dan Kennedy, Jenn Foster and Leading Experts From Around the World.

Video and Social Media Marketing for Professionals: The Top 10 Need to Know Facts for Increasing Local and Internet Traffic.

Video Marketing for Veterinarians: 7 Marketing Strategies to Attract New Clients

Books to Bucks: The Top 20 Ways to Make Money from Your Book (Even if you haven't written it yet)

Book Writing Bible: Expert Secrets on How to Write, Sell, & Market Your Book Online

To receive a special gift and get more information text your name and email to 1-(832) 572-5285.

We are happy to publish your book for you. We will create your book cover and do all the technical stuff and heavy lifting for you. All you do is write the book. Simply Call to order at 1-(832) 572-5285.

Book Writing Retreats - Visit
www.HotChicksWriteHotBooks.com

COMING SOON: Look for our Workbook that we use on our book writing retreats: The Book Writing Fast Pass Workbook.

Subscribe to our Podcast on iTunes - Look for Hot Chicks Write Hot Books
http://0s4.com/r/BOOKS

Subscribe to our YouTube Channel where we interview #1 Best Selling Authors on their successful writing secrets and expert business skills.
http://0s4.com/r/ELITE

Elite Online Publishing is The Brand Building Publisher. We help busy entrepreneurs, business leaders, and professional athletes Create, Publish, and Market their book, to build their business and brand. We are passionate about Authors sharing their stories, knowledge and expertise to help others.

ELITE
Online Publishing